ESSENTIAL ELEMENTS

GUITAR ENSEMBLES

MID INTERMEDIATE

BLUES CRUISE

10 ORIGINAL SONGS WITH BLUESY CHORDS, RHYTHMS, AND RIFFS

by Dave Rubin

ISBN-13: 978-1-4234-1913-6
ISBN-10: 1-4234-1913-8

HAL•LEONARD®
CORPORATION

7777 W. BLUEMOUND RD. P.O. BOX 13819 MILWAUKEE, WI 53213

In Australia Contact:
Hal Leonard Australia Pty. Ltd.
4 Lentara Court
Cheltenham, Victoria, 3192 Australia
Email: ausadmin@halleonard.com.au

Visit Hal Leonard Online at
www.halleonard.com

PREFACE

To explore the scope of the blues, you'd need to start a road trip in Clarksdale, Mississippi, preferably in a 1957 Cadillac. Head northeast to Memphis, pull a U-turn and go southwest to New Orleans before wending northwest to Houston, then due north to Kansas City, continuing up through the Midwest to Chicago and Detroit. Finally, hang a sharp left to end up on the coast of California. What you would find is that—far more than being demarcated by prewar and postwar, or acoustic and electric—the blues is defined by the various regions around the country where it flourished.

The official birthplace of the blues is Mississippi, where the deep 12-bar Delta blues of Charlie Patton and Robert Johnson, along with the later modal Hill Country blues of Junior Kimbrough and R.L. Burnside, originated. Memphis has contributed to many styles, including soul music as purveyed by the Stax artists Booker T & the MGs that springs from the blues and gospel. New Orleans, with its mix of different indigenous music, produced a syncopated groove heard in the songs of Professor Longhair and Fats Domino. Houston and its legends like Albert Collins absorbed the shuffle and made it a Texas specialty like spicy Mexican food. In Kansas City, the blues and jazz intermingled unimpeded and created a swinging subgenre via Count Basie and other "territory bands." Chicago, the official "home of the blues," nurtured a variety of approaches including the Delta-influenced Southside slide style of Muddy Waters and Elmore James and the dramatic West Side style of Magic Sam and Otis Rush. John Lee Hooker made Detroit his home and the boogie was born kicking and hollering. The West Coast smoothed the edges off Texans like T-Bone Walker and Gatemouth Brown, who emigrated and developed a jazzy blues sound. Taken together, they provide a grand tour through the magnificent, exciting, and colorful history of blues guitar. Hop on board and enjoy the cruise. You can ride shotgun with your "axe."

–Dave Rubin

CONTENTS

DELTA CATFISH

By Dave Rubin

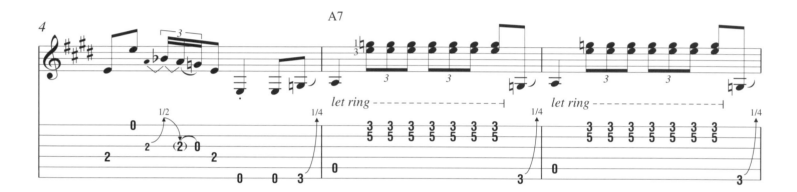

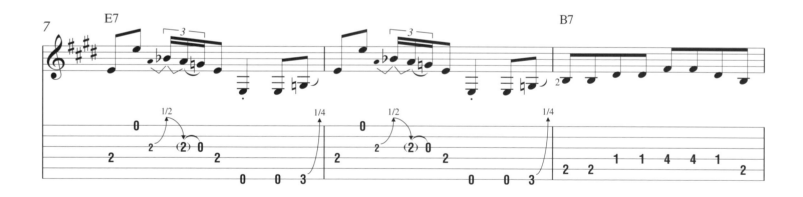

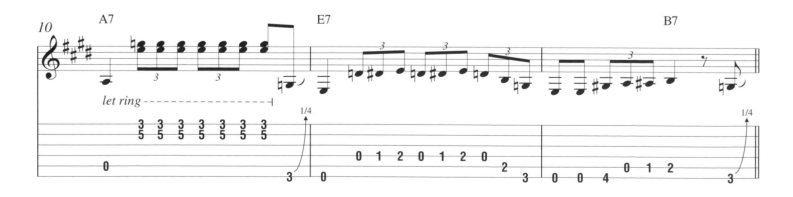

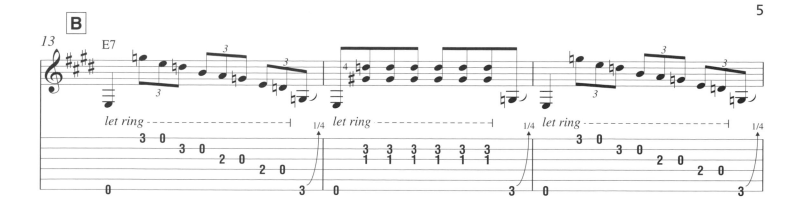

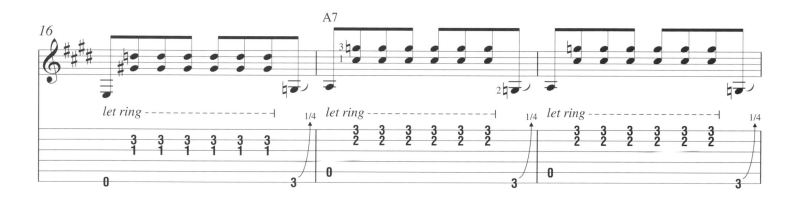

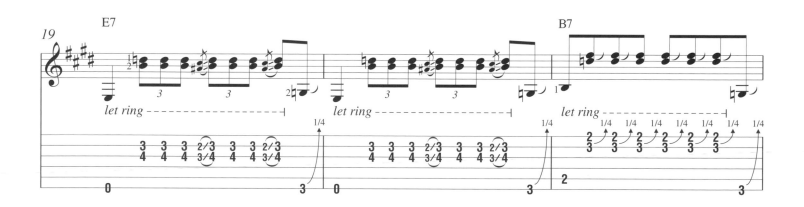

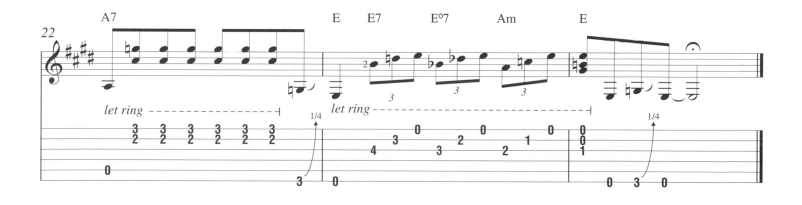

DETROIT BOOGIE

By Dave Rubin

TRACK 2

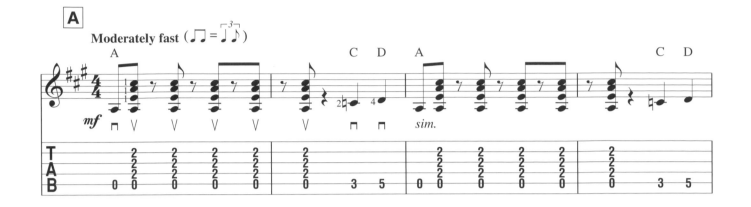

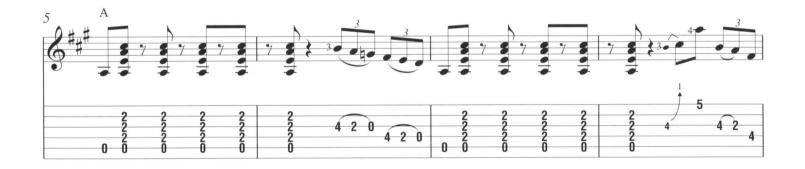

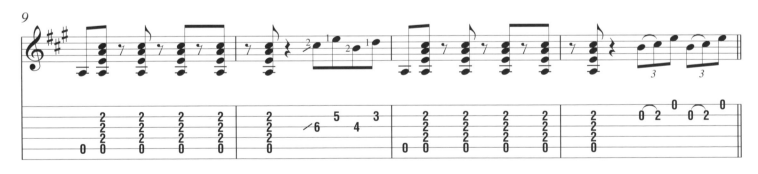

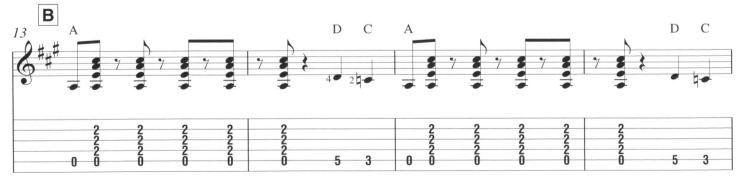

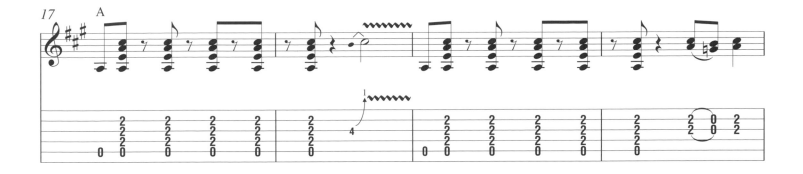

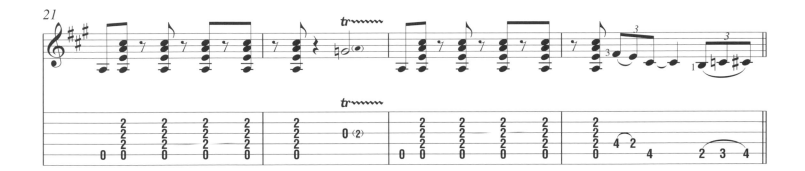

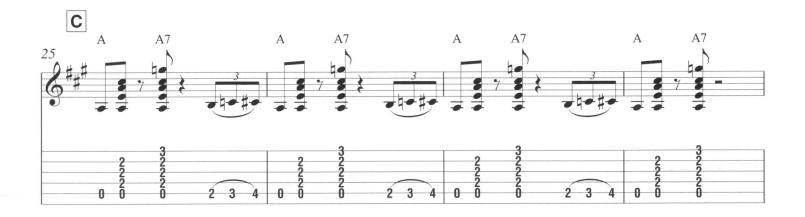

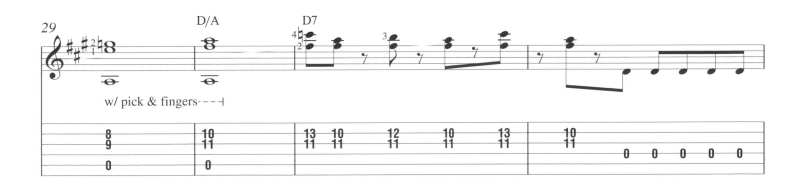

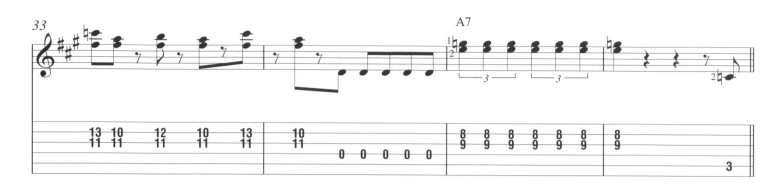

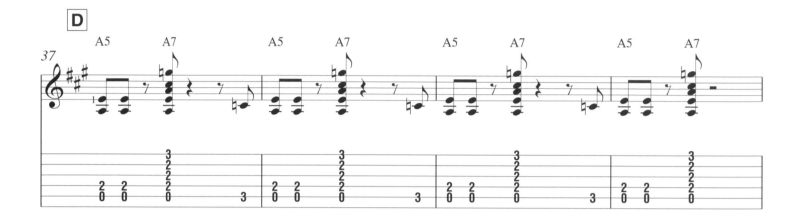

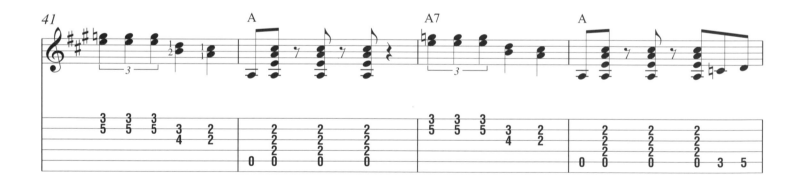

LOUISIANA GUMBO

By Dave Rubin

TRACK 6

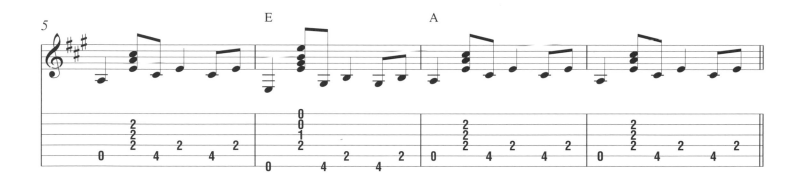

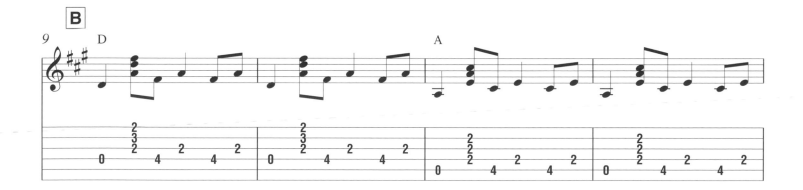

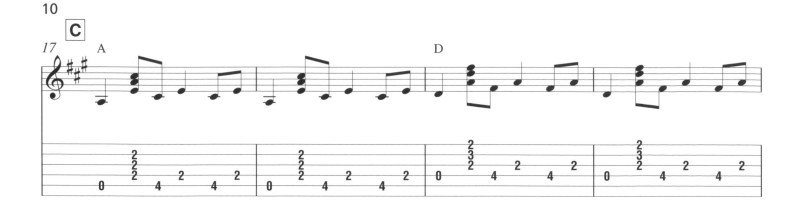

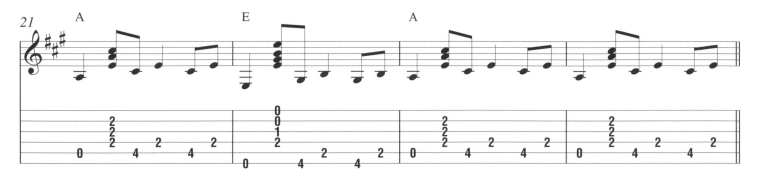

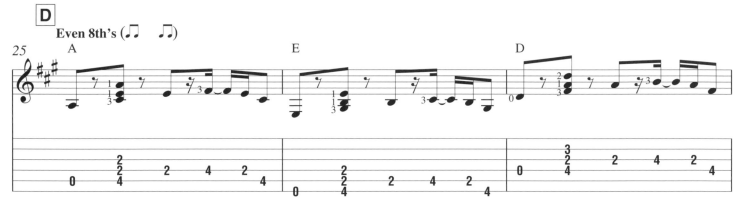

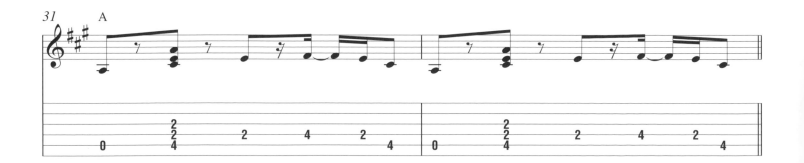

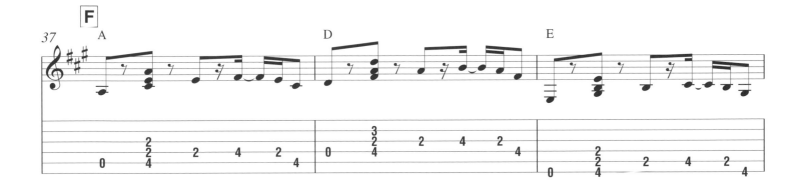

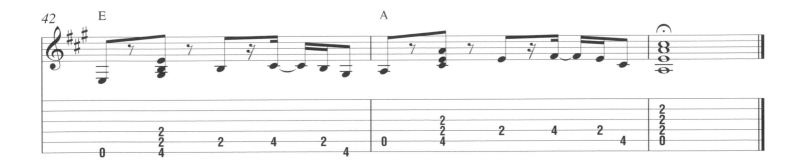

HILL COUNTRY STOMP

By Dave Rubin

TRACK 3

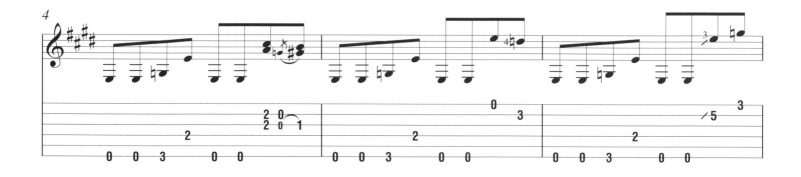

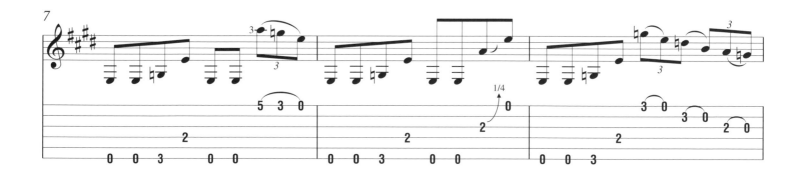

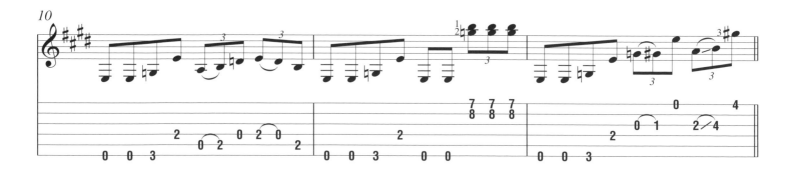

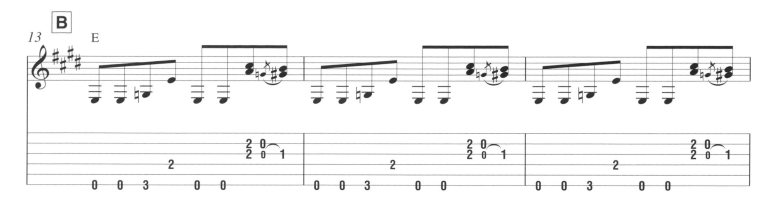

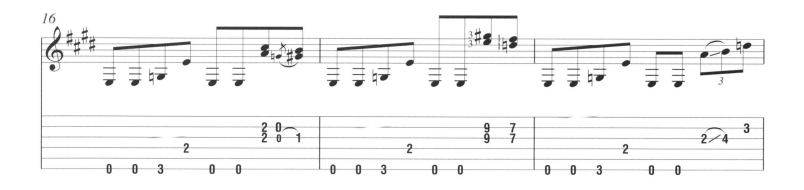

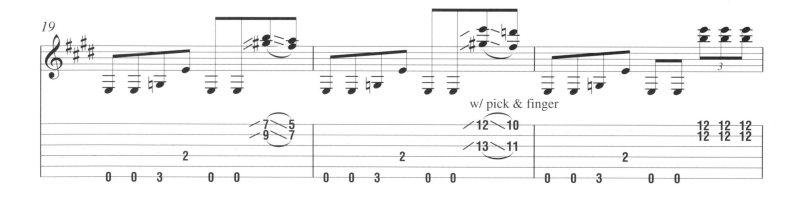

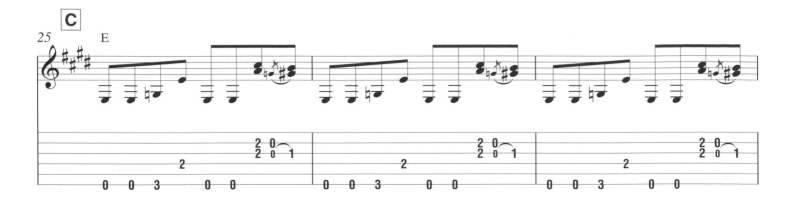

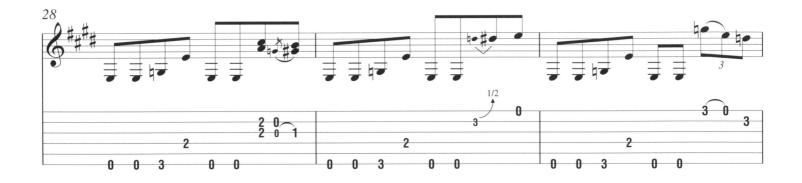

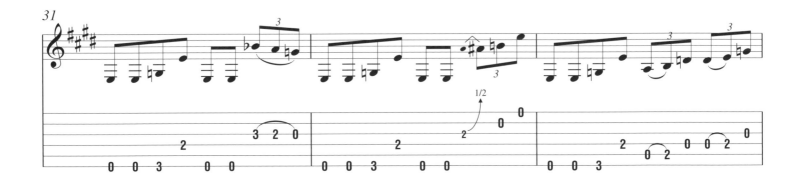

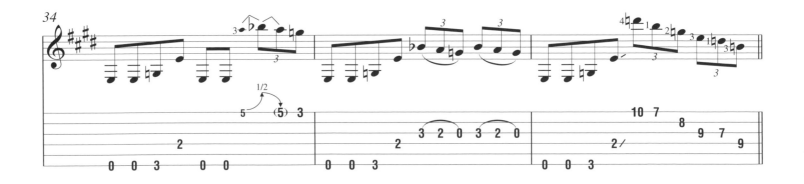

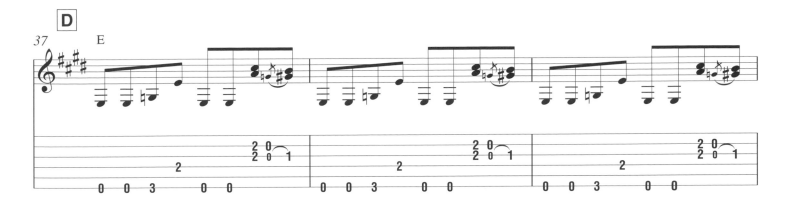

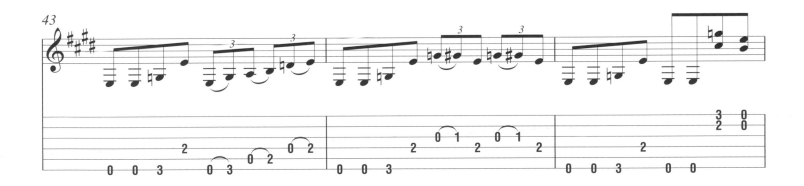

HOUSTON SHUFFLE

By Dave Rubin

TRACK 4

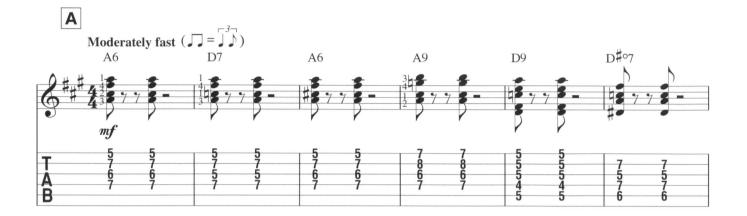

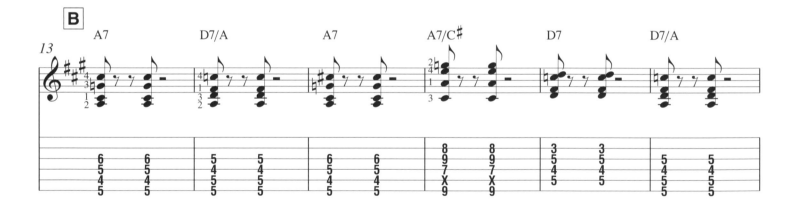

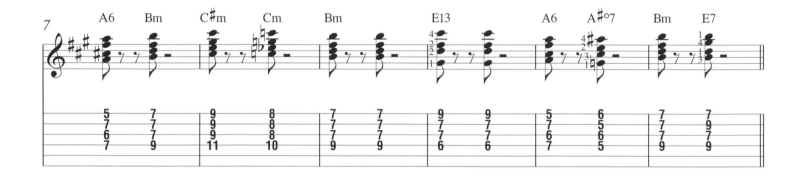

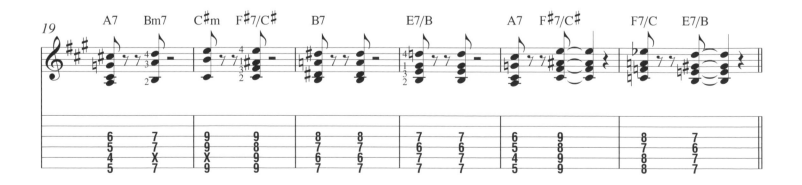

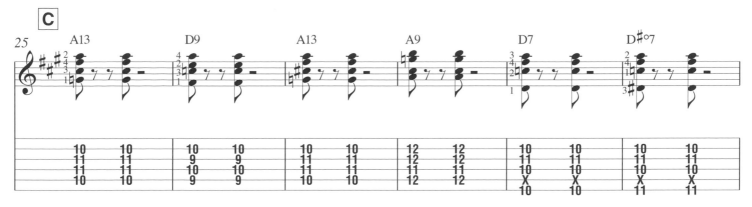

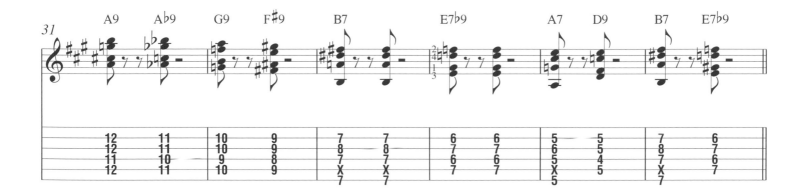

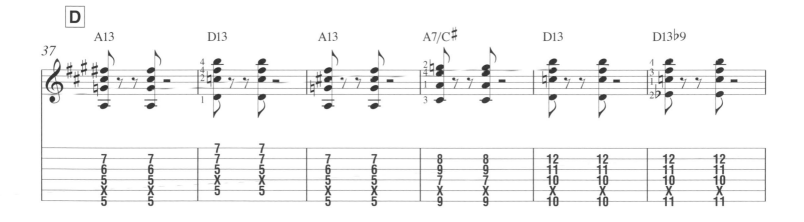

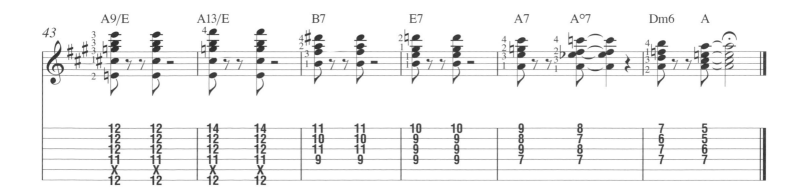

KANSAS CITY SWING

By Dave Rubin

TRACK 5

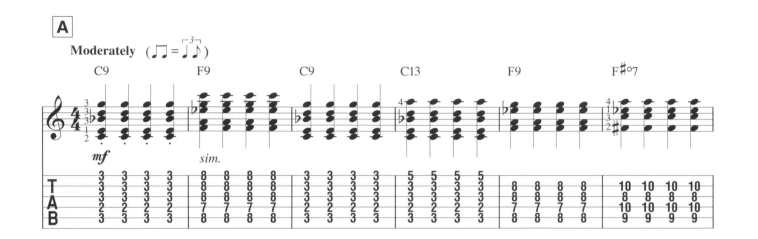

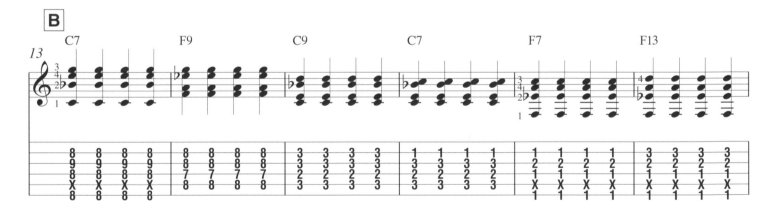

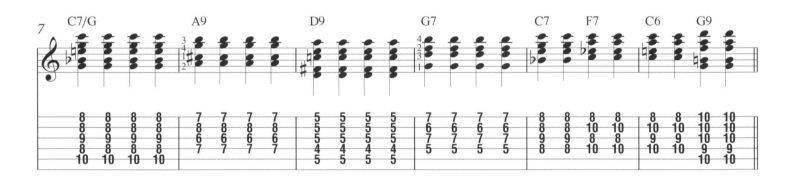

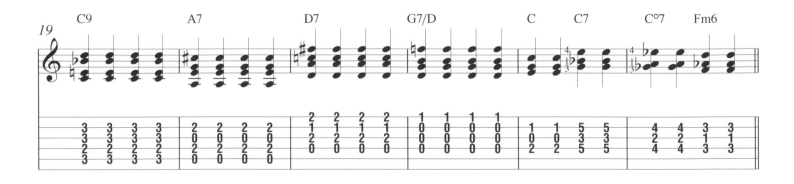

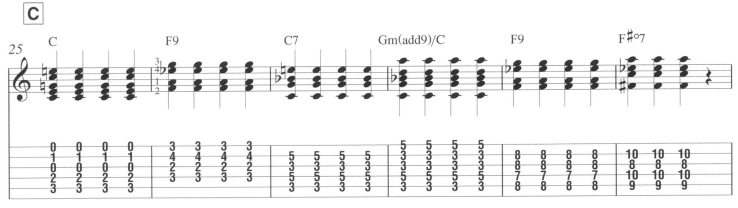

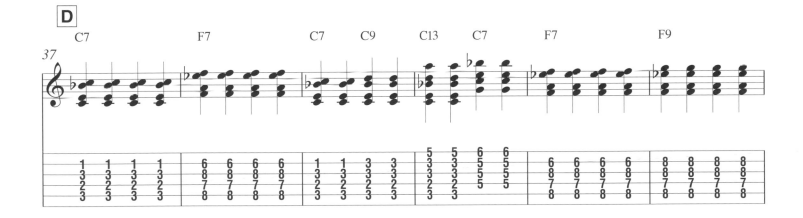

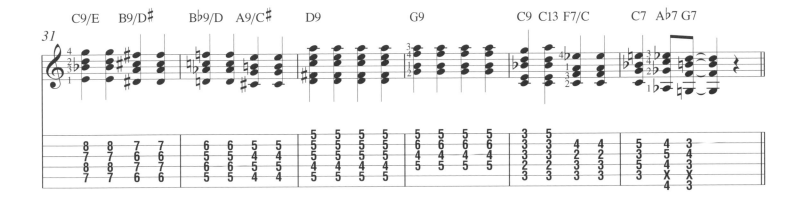

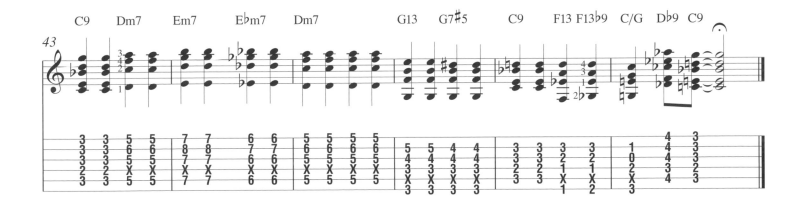

MEMPHIS SOUL

By Dave Rubin

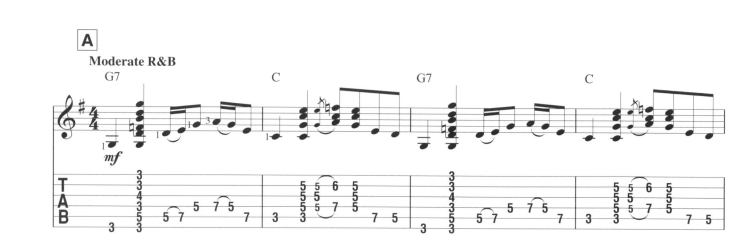

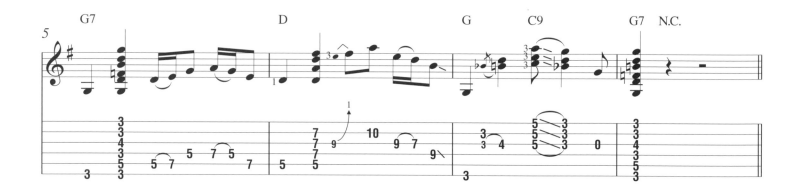

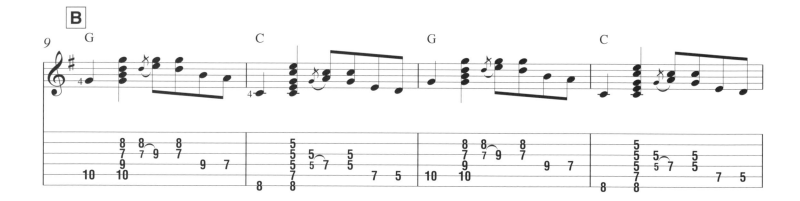

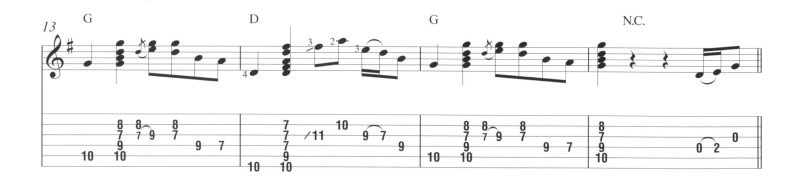

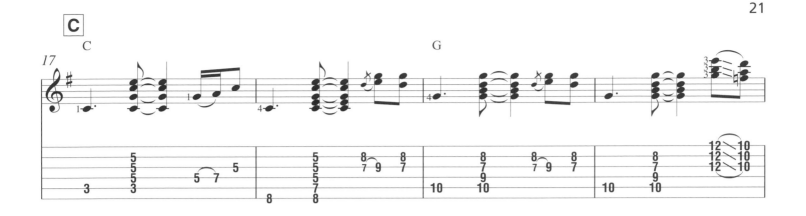

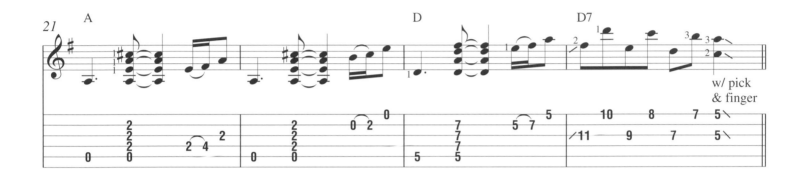

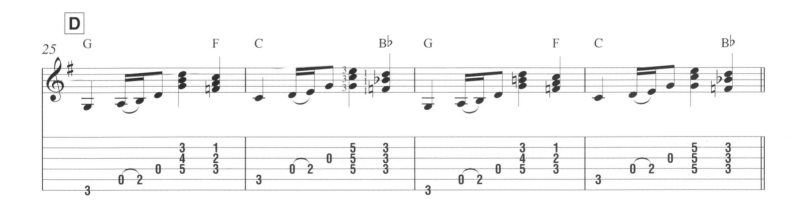

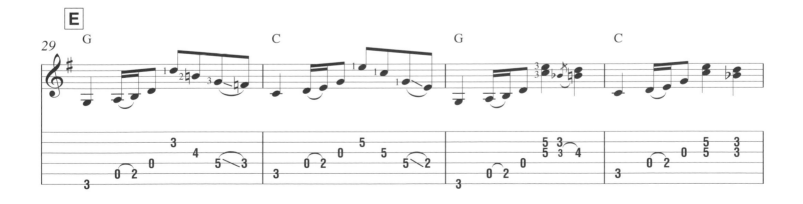

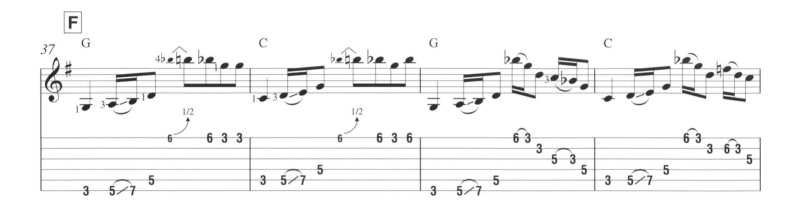

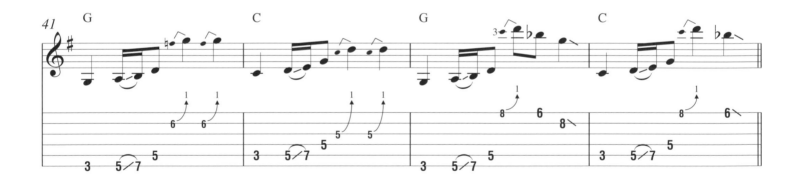

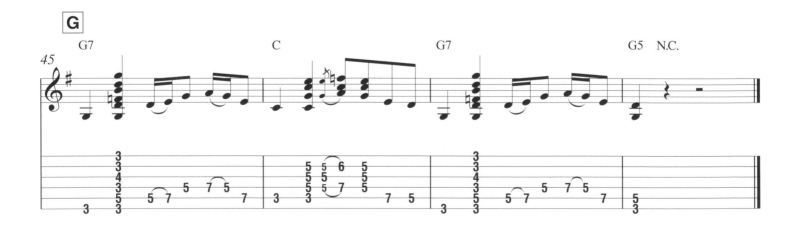

WEST COAST STRUT

By Dave Rubin

TRACK 9

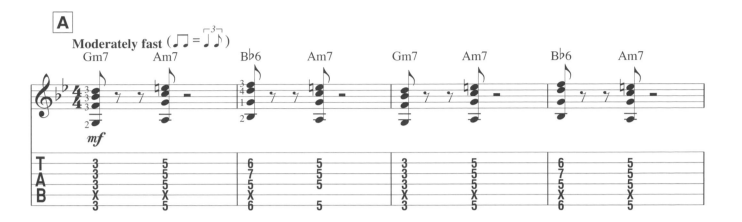

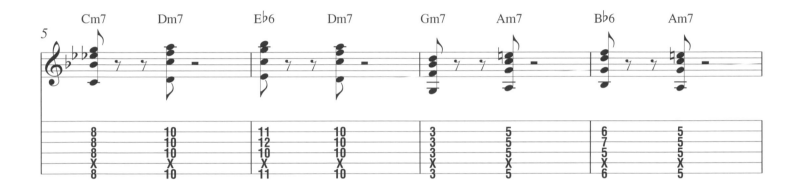

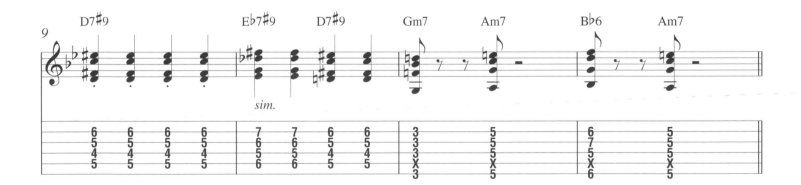

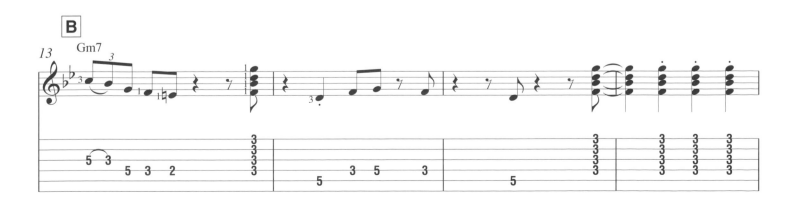

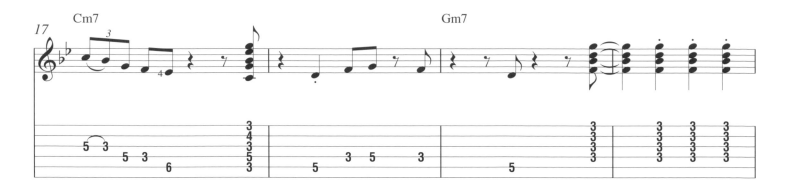

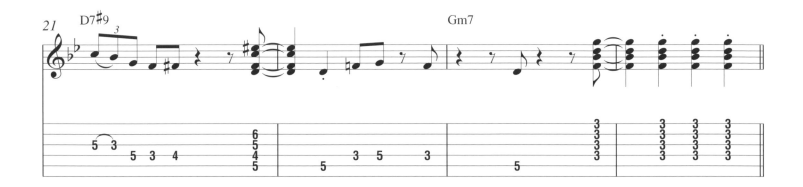

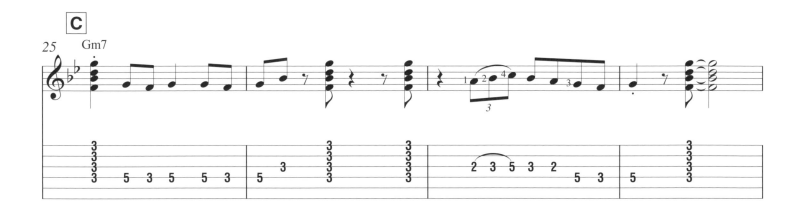

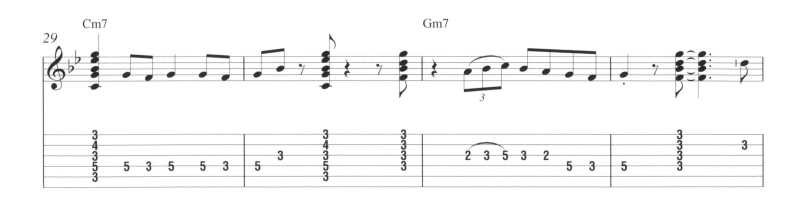

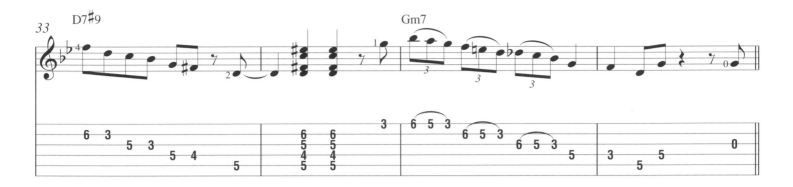

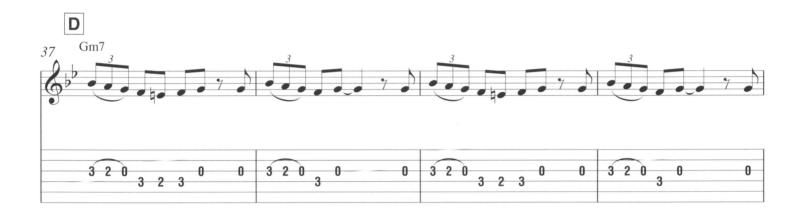

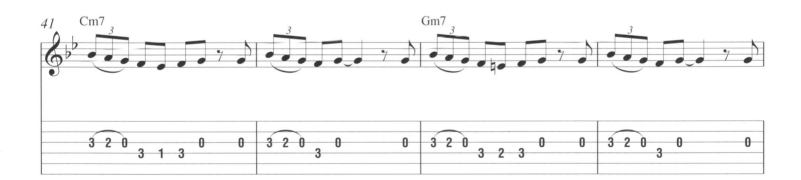

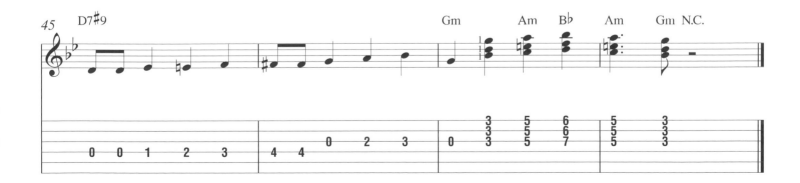

SOUTHSIDE MAN

By Dave Rubin

TRACK 8

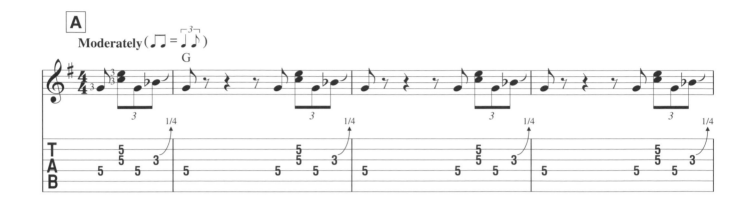

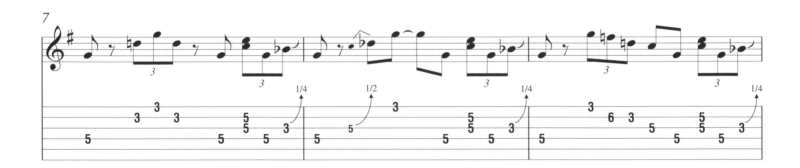

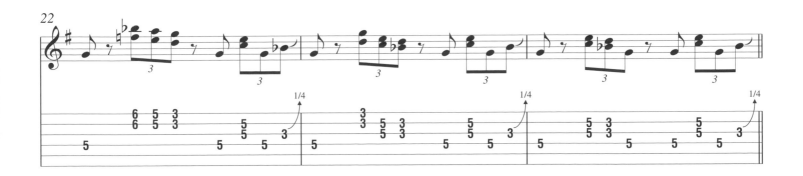

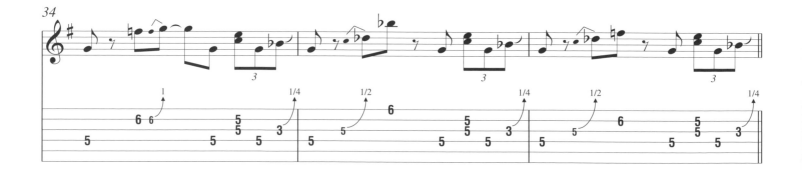

WESTSIDE MINOR GROOVE

By Dave Rubin

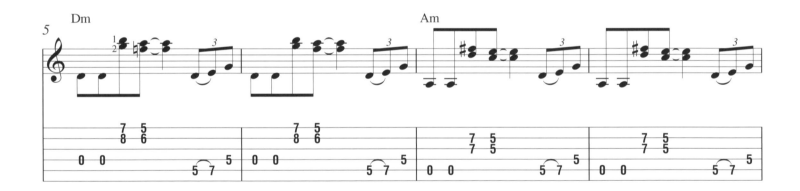

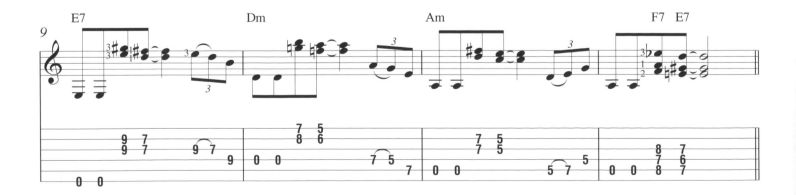

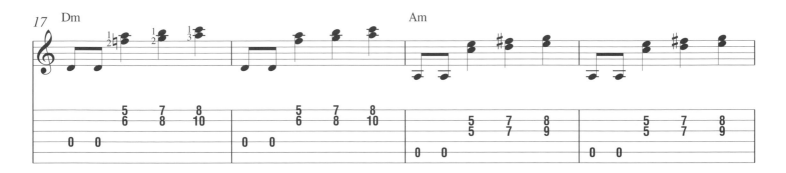

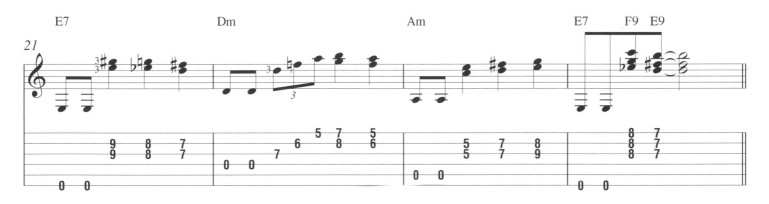

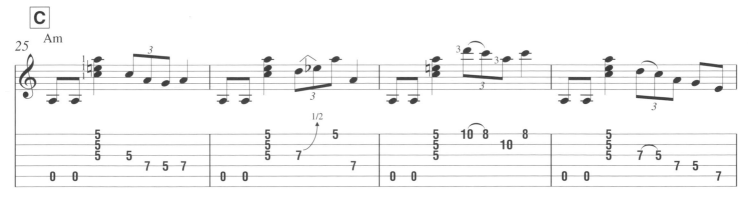

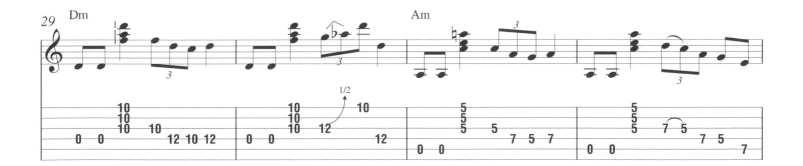

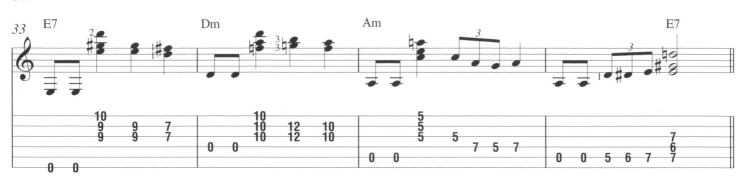

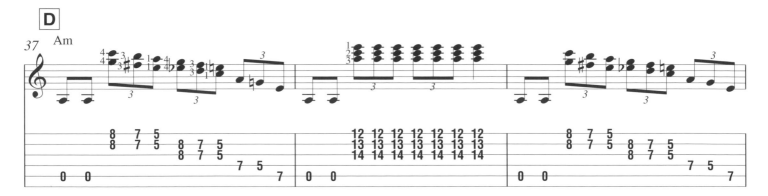

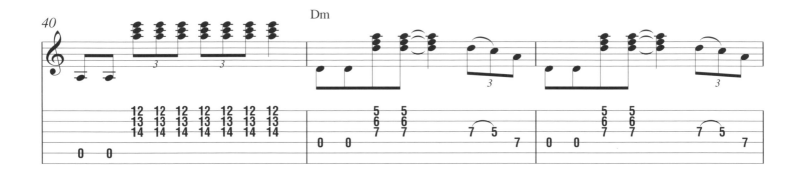

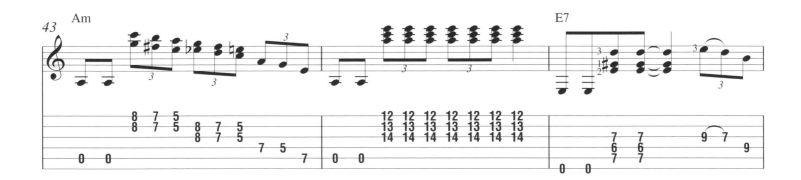

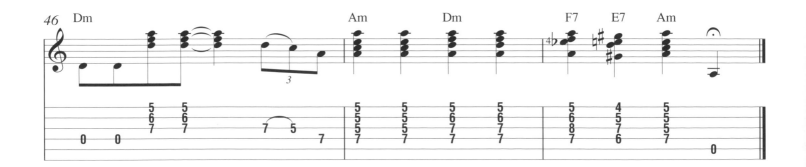